AF283961

Published in 2021 by Search Press Ltd.
Wellwood, North Farm Road
Tunbridge Wells
Kent TN2 3DR

This book is produced by
The Bright Press, an imprint of the Quarto Group,
The Old Brewery, 6 Blundell Street,
London N7 9BH, United Kingdom.
T (0)20 7700 6700
www.QuartoKnows.com

© 2020 Quarto Publishing plc

All rights reserved. No part of this book, text, photographs
or illustrations may be reproduced or transmitted in any form
or by any means by print, photoprint, microfilm, microfiche,
photocopier, internet or in any way known or as yet unknown,
or stored in a retrieval system, without written permission
obtained beforehand from Search Press.

ISBN: 978-1-78221-997-2

Conceived, designed and produced by The Bright Press,
an imprint of Quarto Publishing plc

For The Bright Press
Publisher: Mark Searle
Creative Director: James Evans
Art Director: Katherine Radcliffe
Commissioning Editor: Sorrel Wood
Managing Editor: Jacqui Sayers
Editor: Abbie Sharman
Designer: Emily Portnoi

Printed and bound in China

MIX
Paper from
responsible sources
FSC® C016973

SKETCH
YOUR BEST SELF

HOW TO DRAW SELFIE-STYLE

AMY BLACKWELL

Search Press

CONTENTS

PART 1: YOUR FACE

PART 2: BEYOND BASICS

INTRODUCTION

BE BOLD AND BEAUTIFUL

Create amazing drawings of yourself and your BFFs
that capture each person's character and style.

A night with your friends isn't complete without a selfie, but
unplugging and capturing some of these special moments on
paper can be much more fun. Just a sprinkling of creativity can
bring you and your friends to life on the page and give you
something you'll want to keep forever.

This book is full to the brim with bold, quirky and fun portraits
to inspire you to draw the people in your life in a creative and
personal way. Learn to draw yourself and your friends as you
are every day, or put your imagination to the test with flower
crowns for the festival season or some mermaid magic. All you
need to do now is pick who you want to draw!

PART 1: YOUR FACE

Drawing faces is easier than you think.
This chapter will help you master the
basic shapes that make up the outline
of the face and teach you how to draw
the different facial features.

PART 2: BEYOND BASICS

Take an in-depth look at how to capture
different expressions, from smiles to feeling
icky, before moving on to pattern, colour and
style. Finally, have fun with make-up and
give your friends the perfect hair day.

PART 3: ENTIRE SELFIE

This section will guide you through
the different parts of the body before
putting them together into full figures.
Follow the step-by-step instructions to get the
proportions of you and your friends right.

PART 4: SELFIE STYLE

This part is all about experimenting with
your own style and having fun! Draw
yourself as a robot, or style your BFF
as a superhero. Whether you want to be
in monochrome or full colour, there is
something new to try.

Drawing yourself and your BFFs will help you appreciate
and celebrate what makes each of us unique!

AMY BLACKWELL

HOW TO USE THIS BOOK

This book is designed to give you all the tools you need to create beautiful and stylish selfies. Just follow this simple guide.

Each chapter is full of step-by-step instructions, artist tips and tricks and practice pages to fill with your own illustrations.

Work your way through the book section by section to learn the basics and build on these skills in a guided way, with templates for you to use while you get started and build your confidence.

Or, if you're feeling confident, you can flip through to the final section at any time to experiment with great ways to draw the people you know and love, using fun exercises that give you the space to let your imagination run wild.

PART 1
WILL SHOW YOU
HOW TO CONSTRUCT
YOUR FACE.

PART 2
WILL HELP YOU MASTER
YOUR FAVOURITE EXPRESSIONS.

PART 3
WILL SHOW YOU
HOW TO DRAW THE REST
OF YOUR BODY.

PART 4
WILL GIVE YOU LOADS
OF STYLE SUGGESTIONS
AND EXERCISES.

TOOLS

Every artist needs supplies, so here are
a few essentials to help get you started.

EXPERIMENT WITH
DIFFERENT TYPES
OF PAINT TO FIND
YOUR FAVOURITE.

GATHER A RANGE
OF PAINTBRUSHES.

A MOBILE PHONE WILL COME IN HANDY!

KEEP YOUR PENCILS
SHARP FOR ACCURATE LINES.

9

PART 1

YOUR FACE

Let's work through the basics of the face, feature by feature. In this section, you'll find handy ways to easily draw eyes, mouth, teeth, ears and our absolute favourite – the nose.

DRAW YOUR FACE

Faces come in all shapes and sizes. The most common shapes are round, heart-shaped and oval, but there are many combinations. Start by drawing an oval or circle, then subtly draw the cheeks and chin, adjusting your face shape until you are happy with the result. It's common for faces to be a little asymmetrical, so don't worry about drawing a perfect circle.

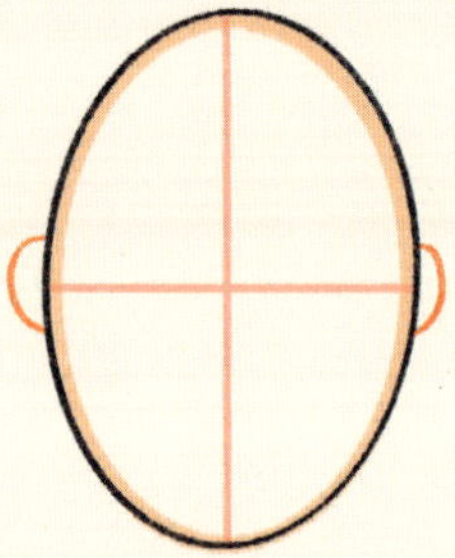

OVAL

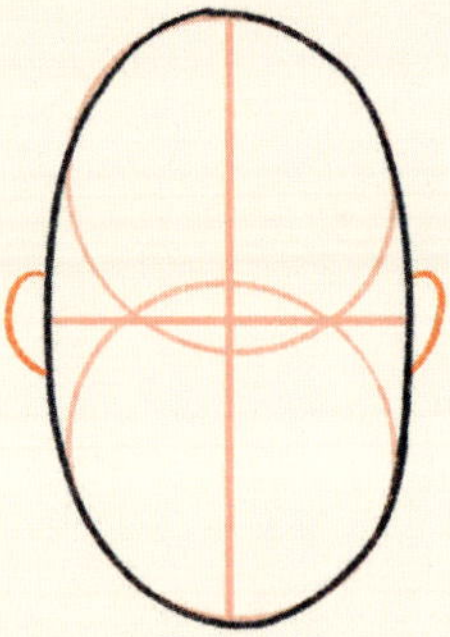

LONG

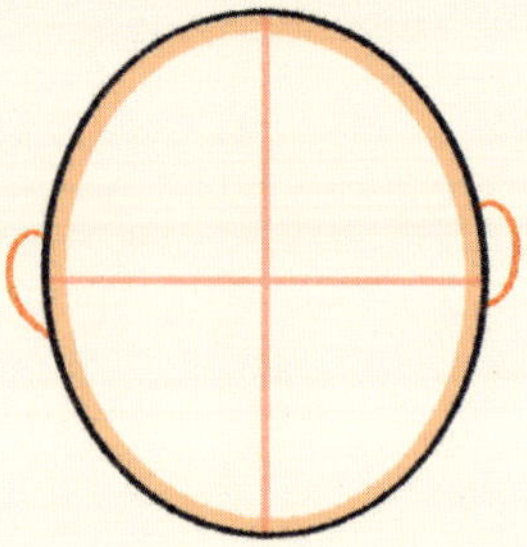

CIRCLE

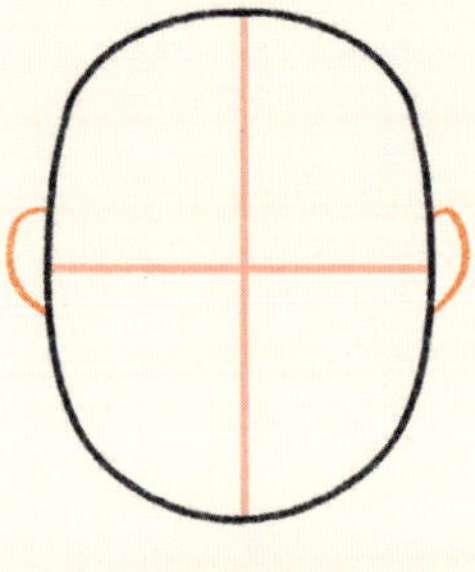

SQUARE

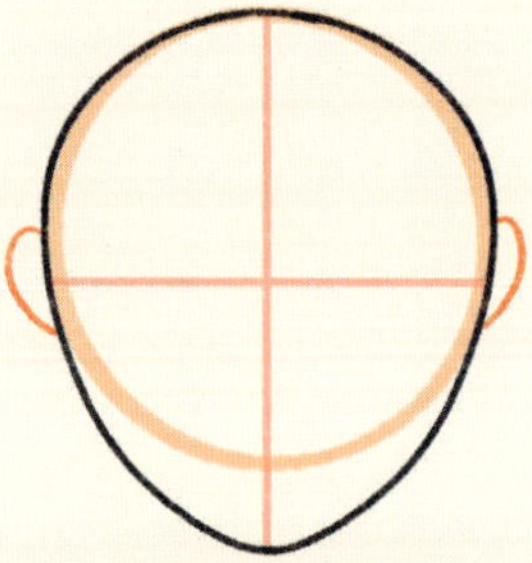

HEART-SHAPED

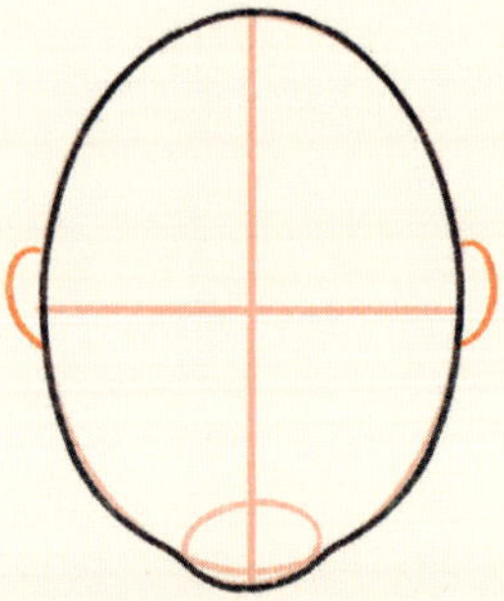

OVAL WITH DEFINED CHIN

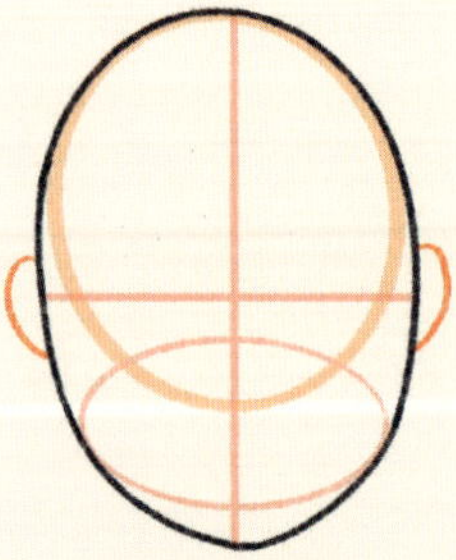

SMOOTH CHIN

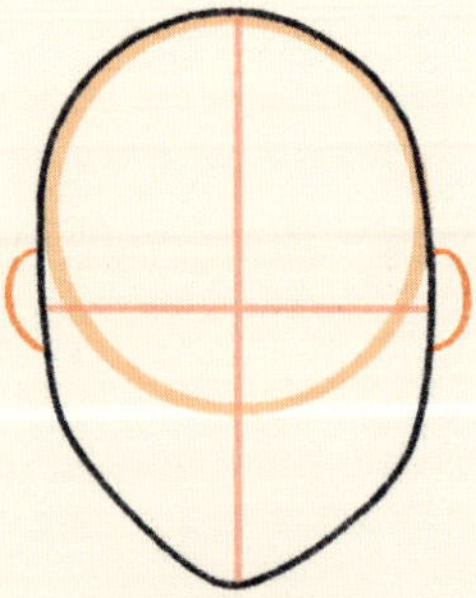

POINTED CHIN

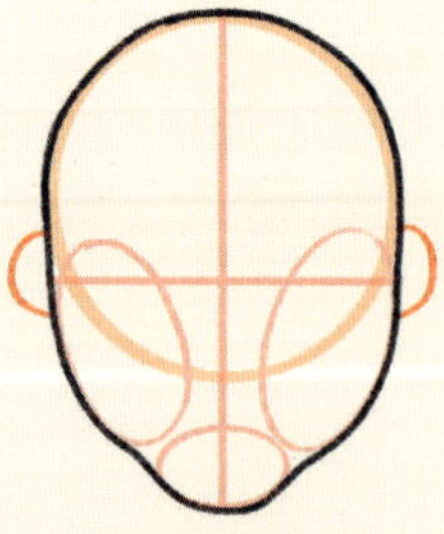

DEFINED CHIN

COMPOSITION

Lightly sketch a guideline down the centre of the face and one across, and use them to position the facial features once you've decided on your face shape.

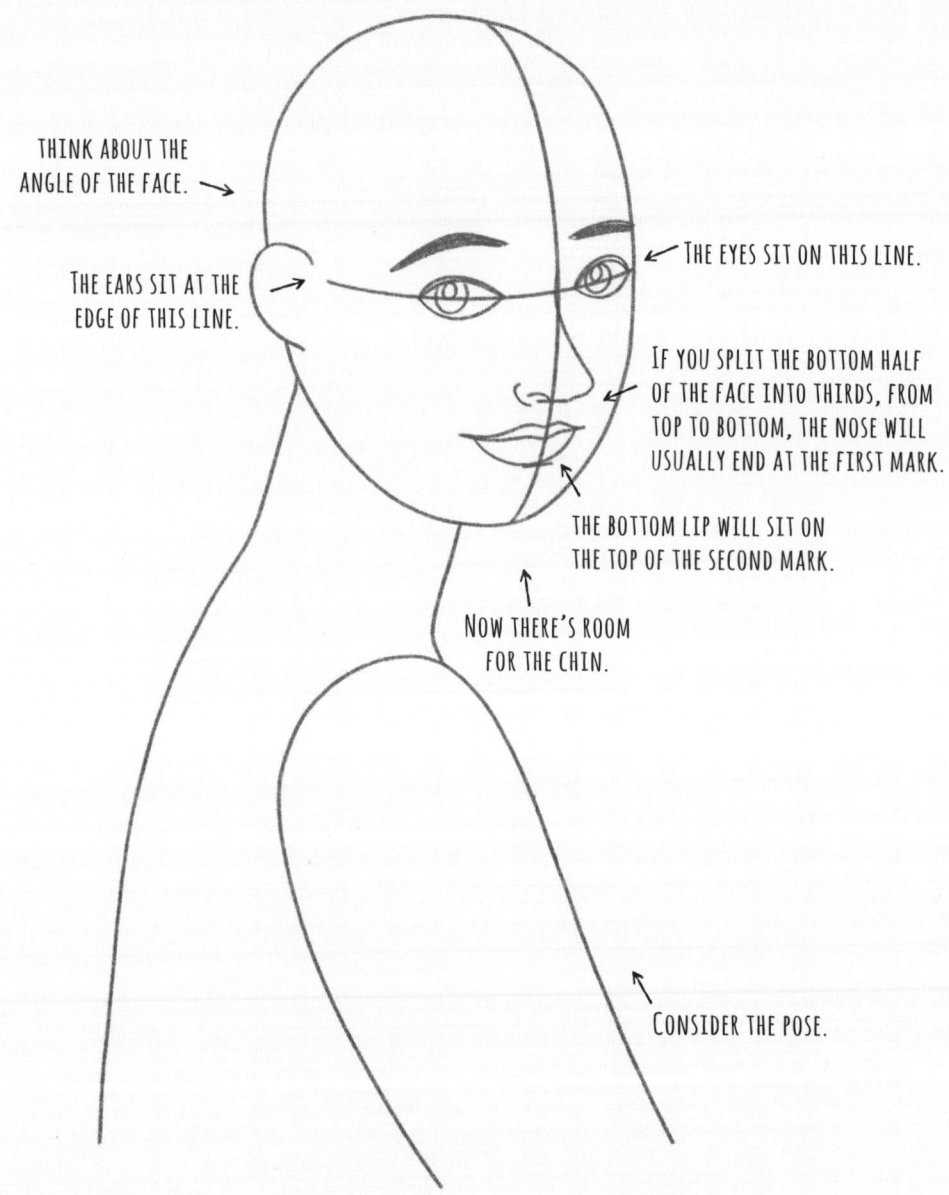

THINK ABOUT THE ANGLE OF THE FACE. →

THE EARS SIT AT THE EDGE OF THIS LINE.

← THE EYES SIT ON THIS LINE.

IF YOU SPLIT THE BOTTOM HALF OF THE FACE INTO THIRDS, FROM TOP TO BOTTOM, THE NOSE WILL USUALLY END AT THE FIRST MARK.

THE BOTTOM LIP WILL SIT ON THE TOP OF THE SECOND MARK.

NOW THERE'S ROOM FOR THE CHIN.

CONSIDER THE POSE.

POSITION YOUR FEATURES

The guideline method of spacing out the features works on averages. Have a look in the mirror and see where your features actually start and where they finish. Note where your eyes sit and how they line up with your ears. Do you have any beauty marks or freckles that might help you lay out your features more accurately?

Up

Left

Face on

Right

Down

ANGLES

Try adjusting the head. To get your angles looking accurate, move the cross of the face into the correct position and line up the chin and top of the head. Adding shading beneath the chin will make your drawings look more realistic.

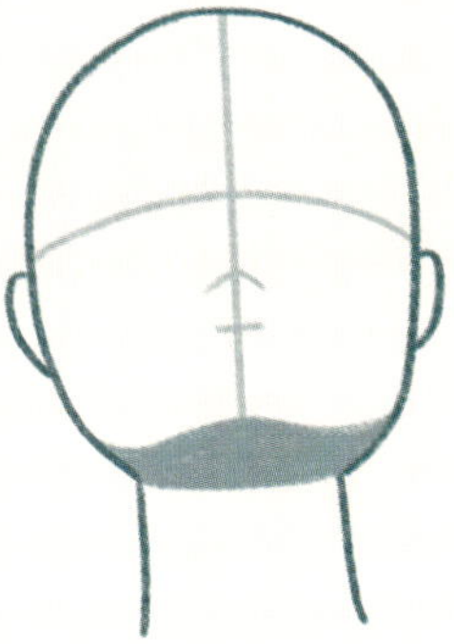

Up

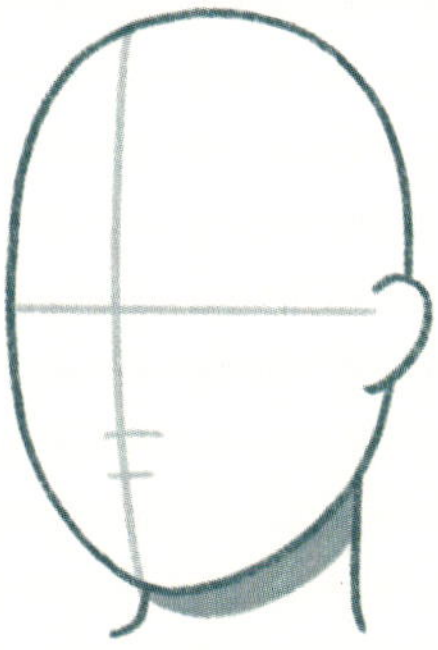

Left

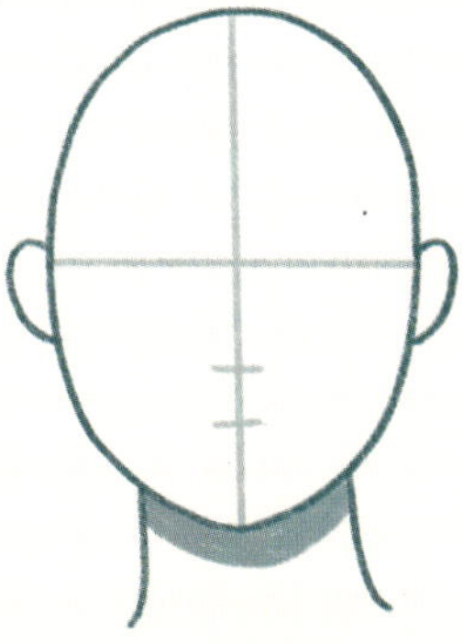

FACE ON

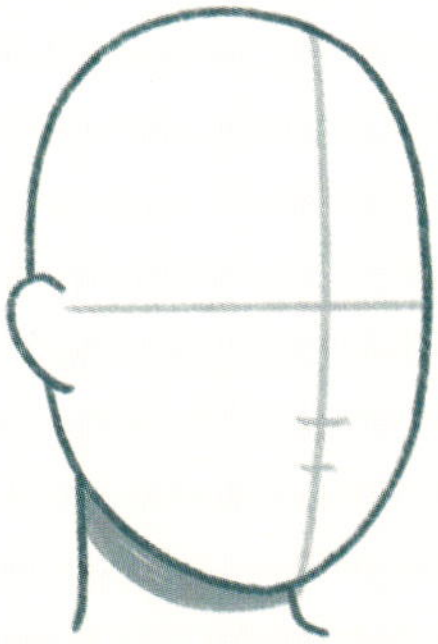

Right

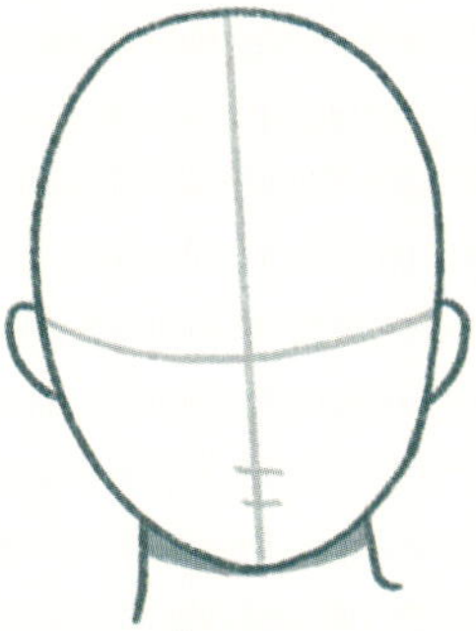

Down

EARS

PLACEMENT

If you look in the mirror, you'll notice that the top of your ear sits at eye level. That will help you place the ears in relation to your other features.

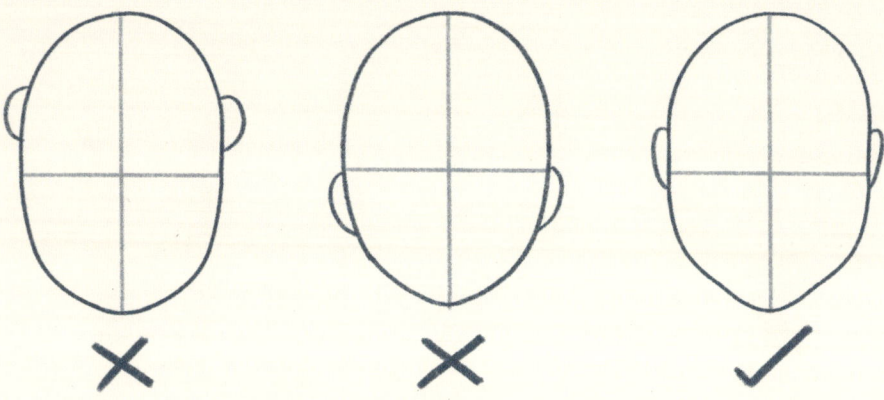

LISTEN UP!

Ears are fun to draw. They come in a few different shapes and, like eyes, can be a little asymmetrical. You can add jewellery to them once you've mastered the basics. Here are some shapes to help get you started.

PAY ATTENTION TO THE SHAPE AT THE TOP OF THE EAR.

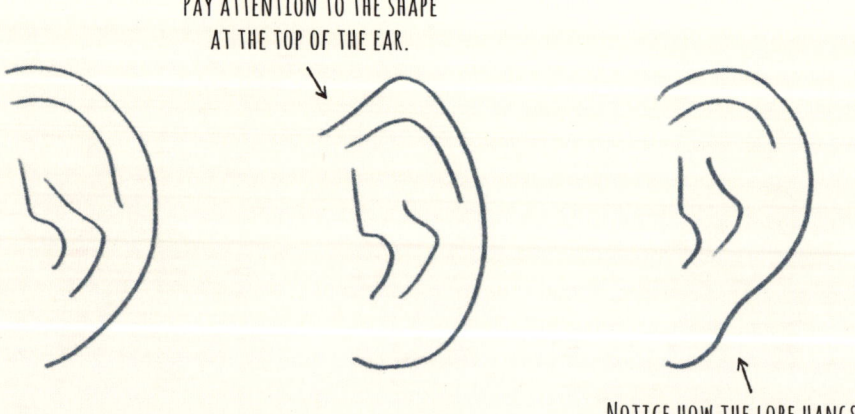

NOTICE HOW THE LOBE HANGS.

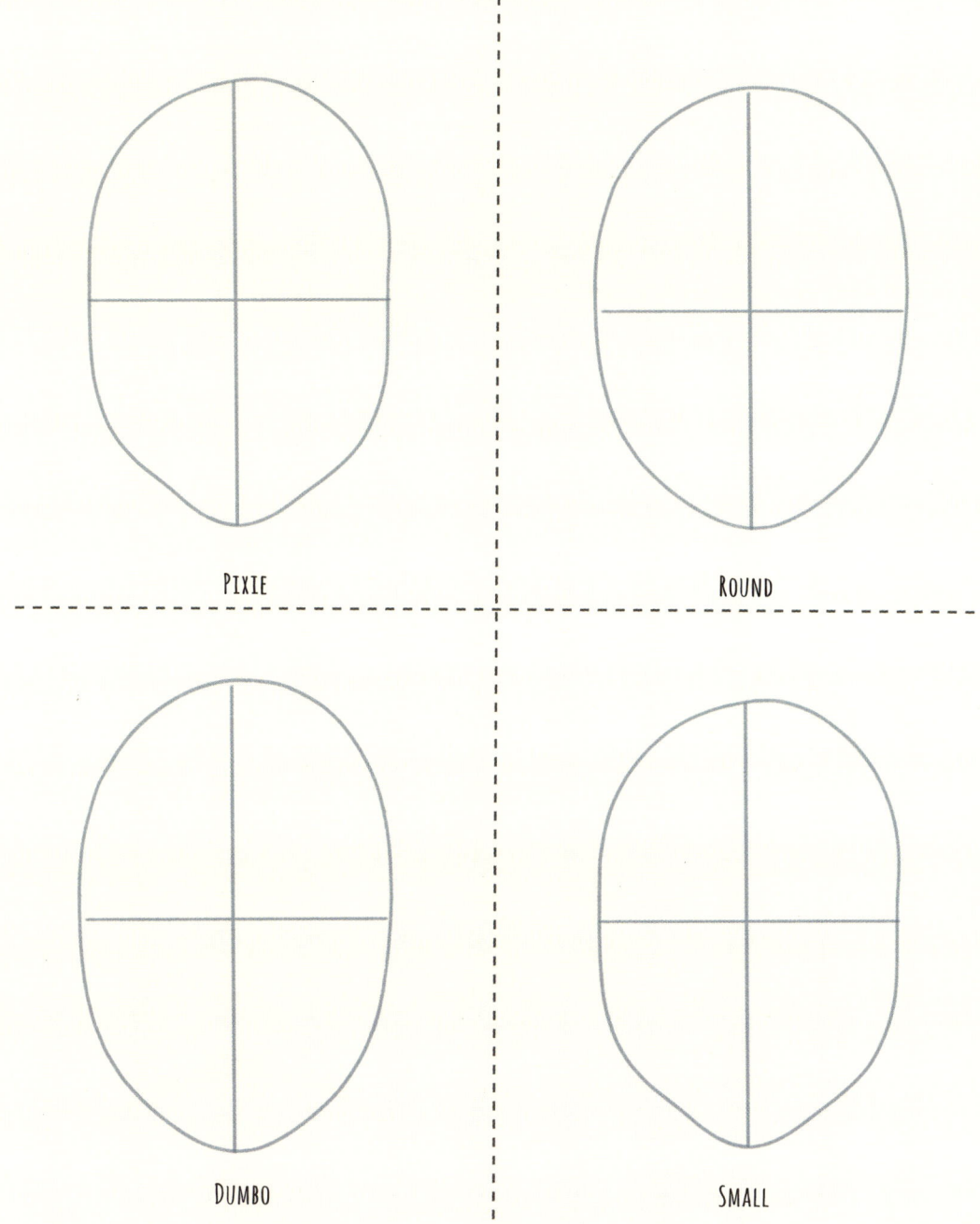

Pixie

Round

Dumbo

Small

19

EYES

PLACEMENT

Surprisingly, eyes sit roughly halfway down the face. Try lining them up with the top part of your ear. The eyebrows should frame the eyes.

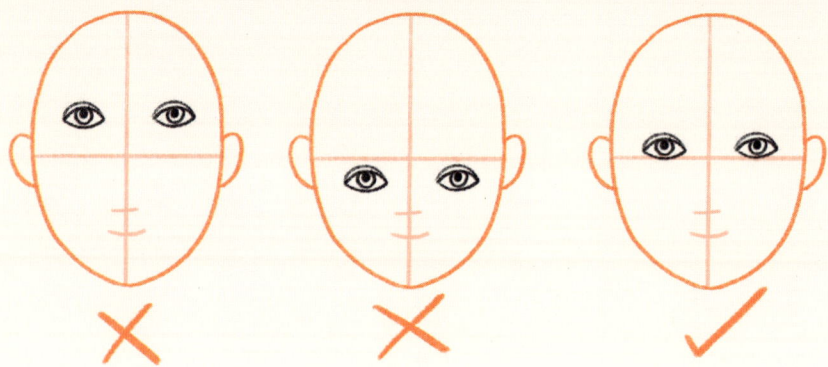

I ONLY HAVE EYES FOR YOU

Starting with the top arch of each eye makes it easier to place the eyes at the right height on your face. Try drawing both eyes at the same time. By drawing each stage of the eye for both eyes, you can keep them symmetrical as you go.

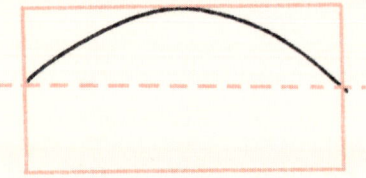

STEP 1:
Begin with the top arch of each eye.

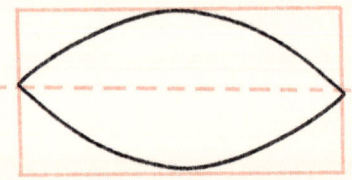

STEP 2:
Draw the bottom line.

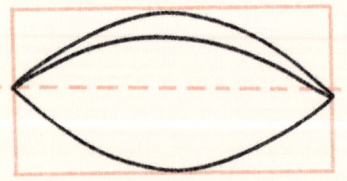

STEP 3:
Create the eyelid.

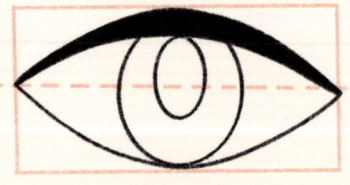

STEP 4:
Add details, including the iris, pupil and a thick lash line.

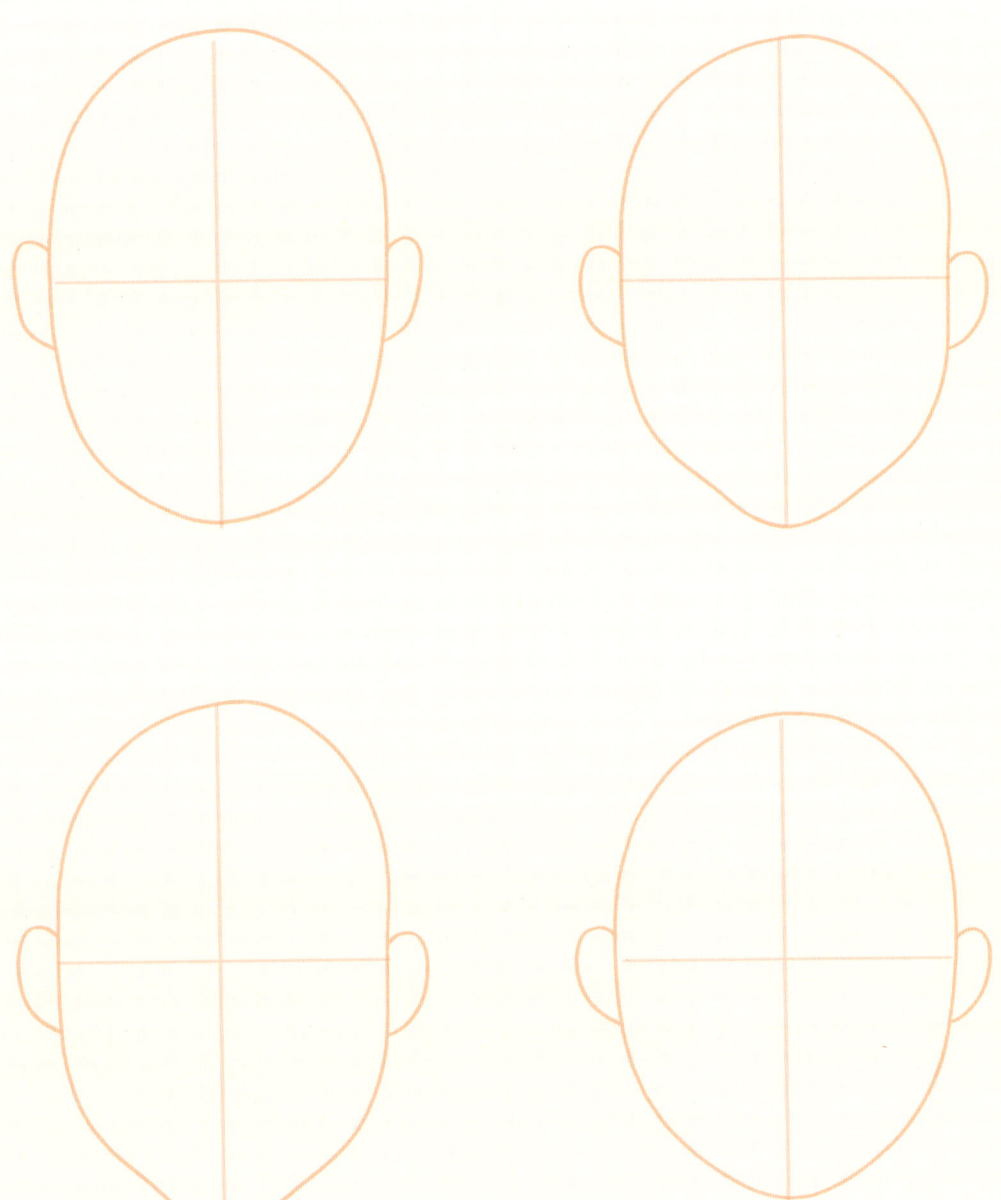

EYE VARIATIONS

To create the eye shapes on the opposite page,
adapt the instructions on page 20.

COMMON EYE SHAPES

Everyone's eyes are different, so try adding some character by experimenting with shapes and eyelids.

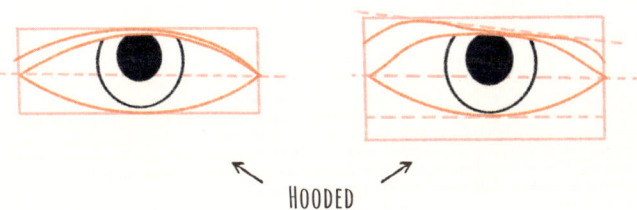

HOODED

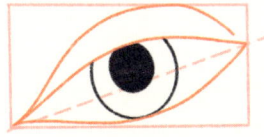

UPTURNED

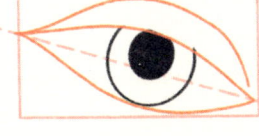

DOWNTURNED

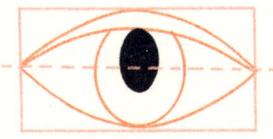

ALMOND

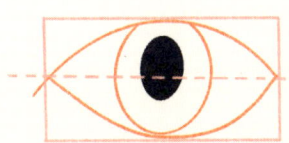

MONOLID

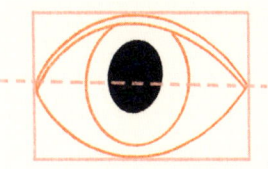

ROUNDED

NOSES

PLACEMENT

Use the examples below to work out the correct placement for your nose. Remember, the bridge of the nose starts between the eyes.

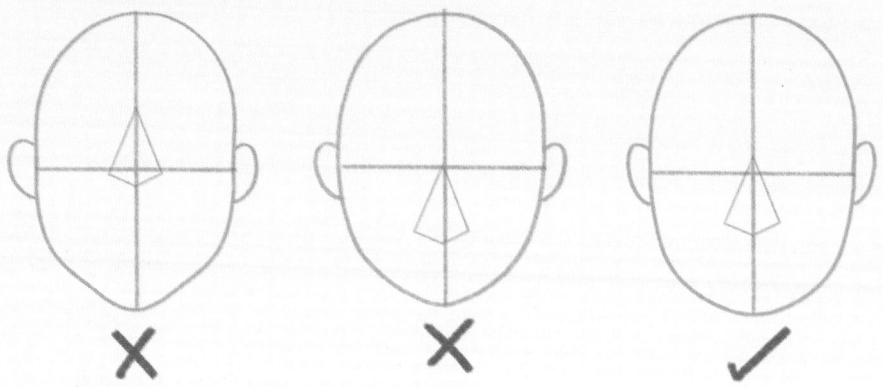

I'VE NOSE DOUBT YOU CAN DO THIS

Ahh, noses. They get a bad rap in the portrait world, but are surprisingly quick and easy to draw. They just take a little practice.

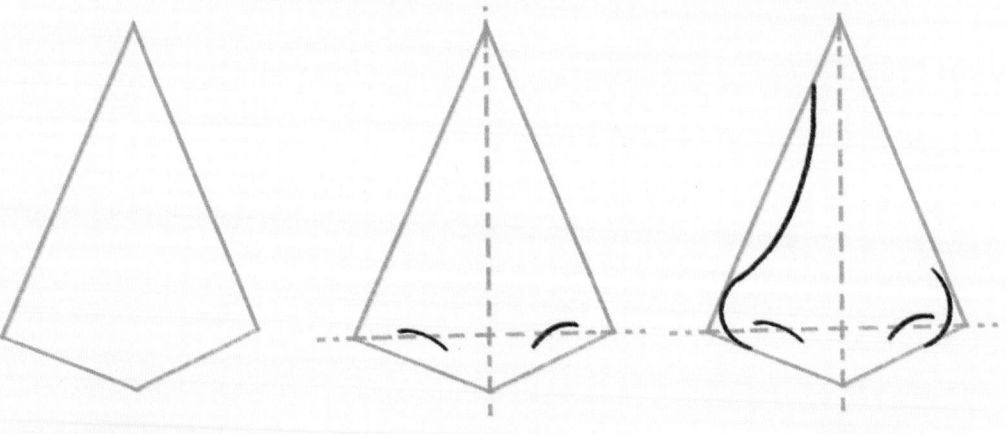

STEP 1:
Start with a pyramid-shaped guide.

STEP 2:
At the bottom of the horizontal line, add some small curves for nostrils.

STEP 3:
Tweak the shape of the nose by playing around with the curved lines at the side and the width between the nostrils.

Draw noses on these faces and add the rest of the facial features.

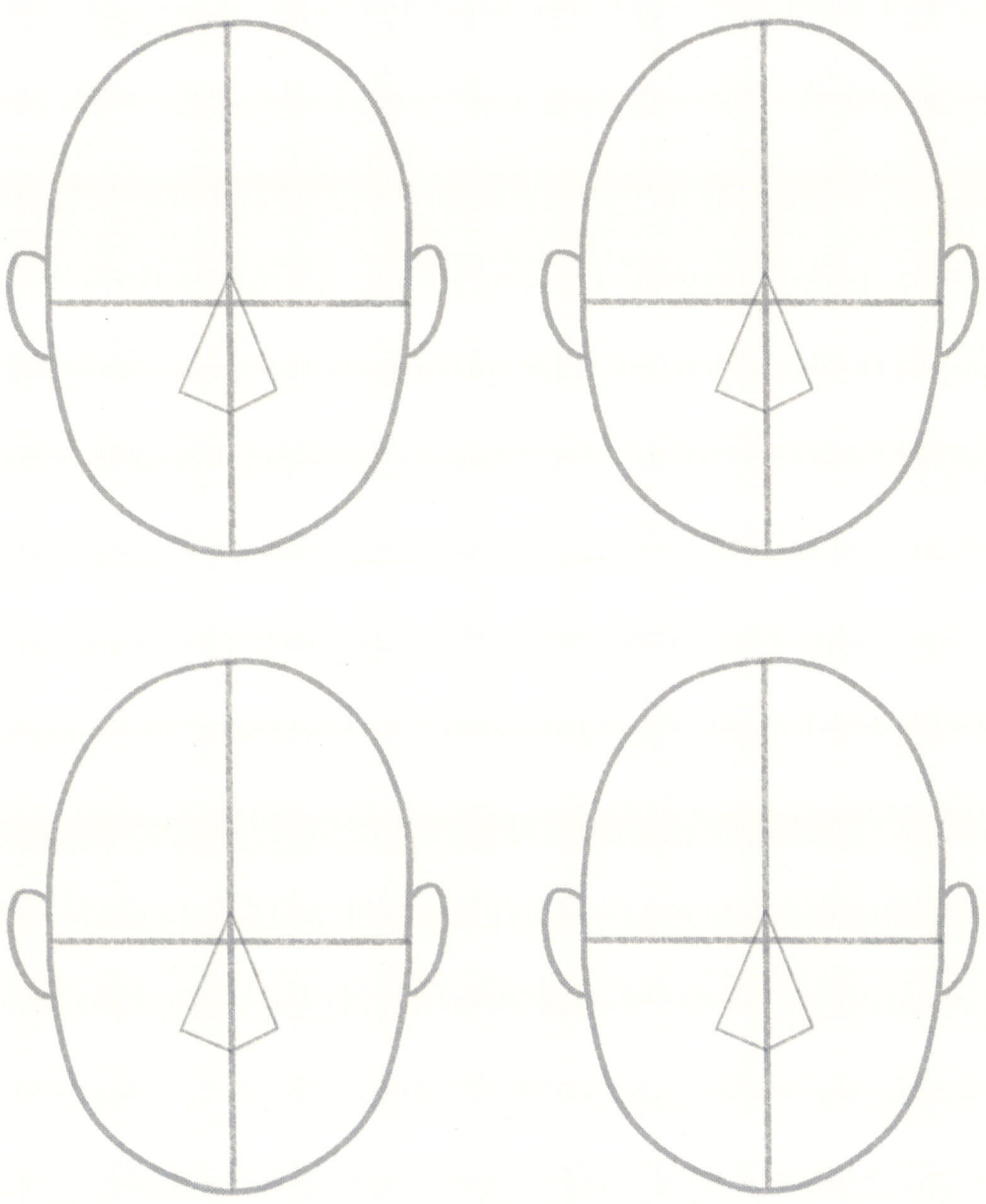

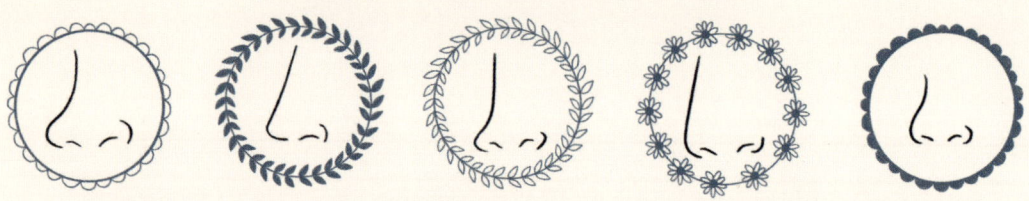

Changing just the nose can radically change the look of your portrait. Have fun experimenting with different sizes and shapes.

A SIDE NOSE

Think about your profile. How much does your nose stick out?
Do you have a ski slope to be proud of or is it as cute as a button?

Pointy nose   Flat nose   Button nose

TRY IT OUT!

MOUTH

PLACEMENT

Using the eye guideline and the tip of the chin will help
you place the mouth in the correct position.

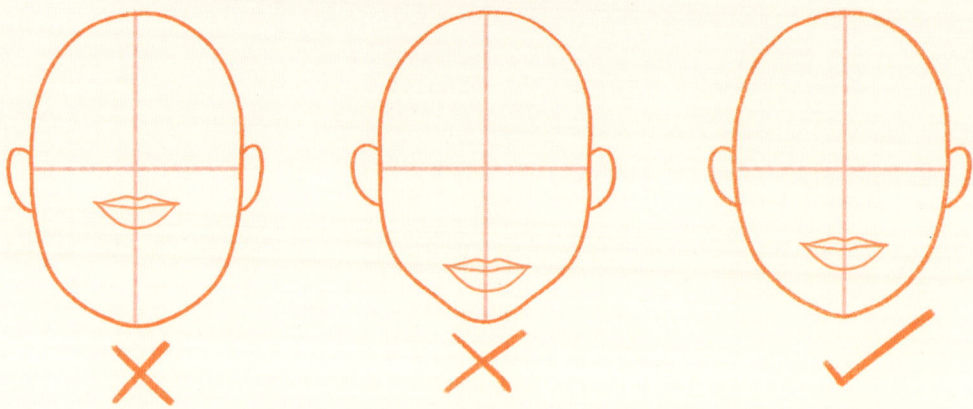

PUCKER UP!

Mouths are my favourite thing to draw. They come in
all shapes and sizes, and you can make them almost any colour.

FULL   POINTY   ROUND   UNI-LIP

STEP 1:
Start with the top lip.

STEP 2:
Next comes the bottom lip.

STEP 3:
Then draw the line
to divide them.

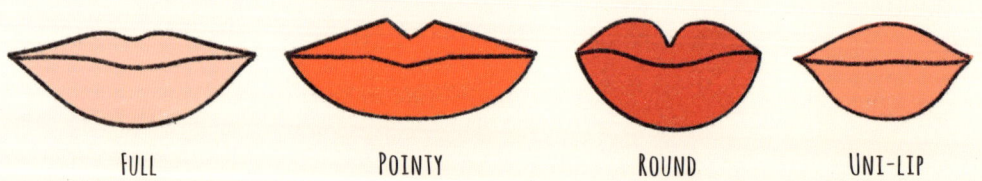

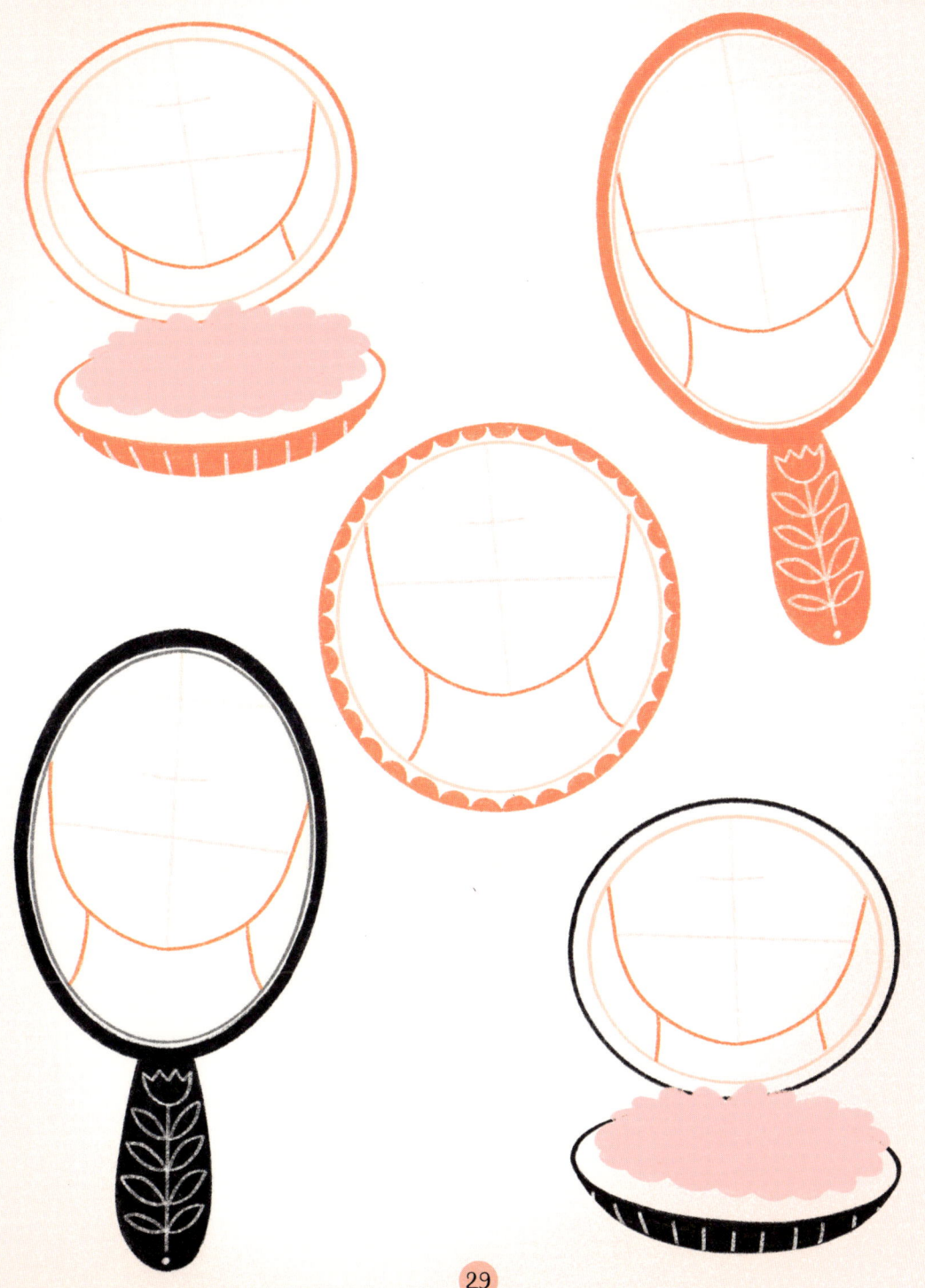

Colour in the lips and add teeth to these mouths.

TEETH

BITE-SIZE STEPS

Drawing teeth can be a little daunting, so keep it simple and limit the amount of detail. For some grins, you might just draw a subtle dividing line for the teeth, but for a super-cheesy smile, adding a darker colour between the two rows gives the perfect open-mouthed grin.

STEP 1:
Pick a guide shape, and mark the bottom of the top lip and the bottom of the lower lip.

STEP 2:
Draw the lip outline.

STEP 3:
Use slightly curved lines to draw two rows of pearly whites.

STEP 4:
Add a darker colour between the teeth.

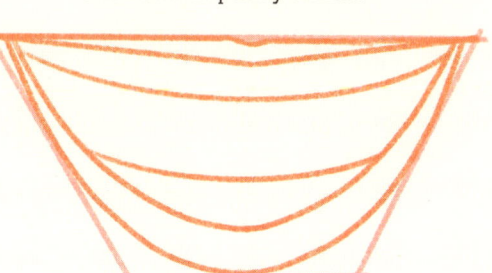

PART 2

BEYOND BASICS

Now we've nailed the face, it is time
to experiment with expressions,
hair, style, colour and pattern.

EXPRESSIONS

Our features change from second to second, with each thought and expression. Let's look at the subtle shifts that give away our emotions.

CLOSED EYES AND A WIDE SMILE

LAUGHING

LIDS AND BROWS SIT LOW

SAD

USE A DOT FOR THE MOUTH

SURPRISED

GAZING OFF TO THE SIDE

BORED

WIDE EYES AND A THIN MOUTH

SCARED

TOOTHY GRIN AND BIG EYES

EXCITED

WIDE EYES AND RAISED EYEBROWS

SHOCKED

EYES FORM A SLIGHT CRESCENT

PLEASED

GAZE SHIFTS UPWARD

THOUGHTFUL

DRAW YOURSELF WHEN...

YOU'RE TOLD A SECRET

YOU'RE SETTING OFF FOR A VACATION

YOUR CRUSH JUST TEXTED

YOU'VE LOST YOUR PHONE

IT'S FRIDAY NIGHT

IT'S MONDAY MORNING

DRAW YOURSELF...

Puckering up!

Giving a sneaky smile

Sticking out that tongue!

Saying 'CHEESE!' with a big grin

ALL SMILES

PUCKER UP!

BIG GRIN

SNEAKY SMILE

SUPER SASS

CROOKED SMILE

LITTLE SMIRK

LOL

TOOTHY SMILE

HAPPY SURPRISE

GRUMPY ME

FEELING ICKY

STRESSED

WTF!!

STEWING

ANNOYED

INSECURE

DISGUSTED

COMPLAINING

CONCERNED

WORRIED

CREATING STYLE

Now you can draw expressive faces, let's think about adding some clothing to your portrait. Just a hint of a neckline or the top of a T-shirt can help give your selfie some style.

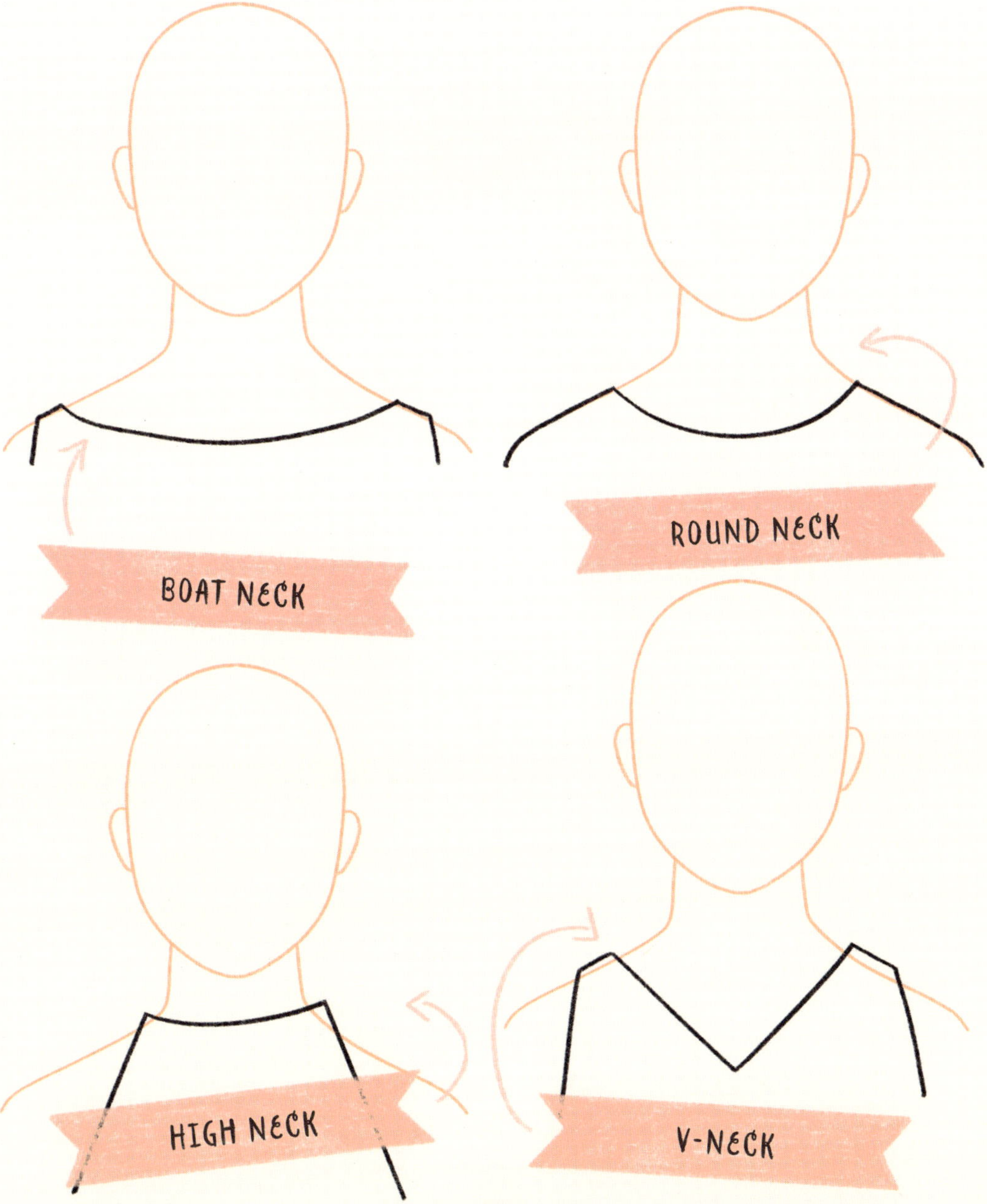

BOAT NECK

ROUND NECK

HIGH NECK

V-NECK

 # USING PATTERN

Brighten up the clothing in your portrait and add some personality to the background with pattern.

FILL THESE SELFIES WITH PATTERN

USING COLOUR

Playing around with colour combinations is one of my
favourite things to do. Once you have the face shape and
layout down, you can start adding whichever colours you fancy.
Try true-to-self colours to illustrate and add depth to your portrait
or go wild and abstract. My advice would be to use contrasting
colours, so your features and details really pop.

Same drawing,
different colours!

MY MAKE-UP LOOKS

MONDAY MORNING

FESTIVAL STYLE

THE 'GO TO' LOOK

DARK AND MYSTERIOUS, FOR DATE NIGHT

MAKE-UP

Some days au naturel just won't do, so give your
selfie some added glamour, too.

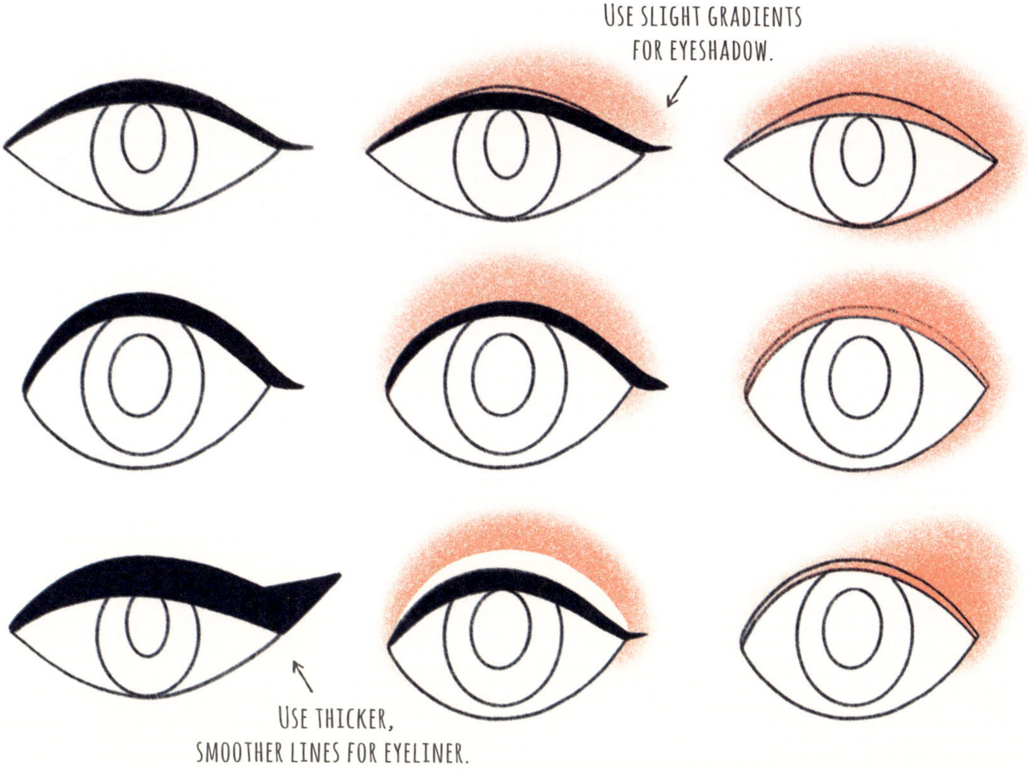

USE SLIGHT GRADIENTS
FOR EYESHADOW.

USE THICKER,
SMOOTHER LINES FOR EYELINER.

USE NEUTRAL COLOURS AND SOFTER EDGES FOR A MORE SHEER LOOK.

GET PARTY-READY
WITH A VIVID RED.

HAIR

STEP 1: Find where your hair parts and mark it with an 'x.' Is your hair symmetrical or off-centre?

STEP 2: Draw the outline of your hair, defining the shape and volume.

STEP 3: Fill in the texture using simple lines and shapes.

MY FAVOURITE DO

GOOD HAIR DAY

When your hair is behaving itself,
it can form pleasing shapes.

RECTANGLE

PIZZA SLICE

ARCH

CIRCLE

TWO CIRCLES

TILTED RECTANGLE

GEOMETRIC

TRIANGLE & CIRCLE

TRIANGLES

Draw hair for these women by using different shapes or combining them.

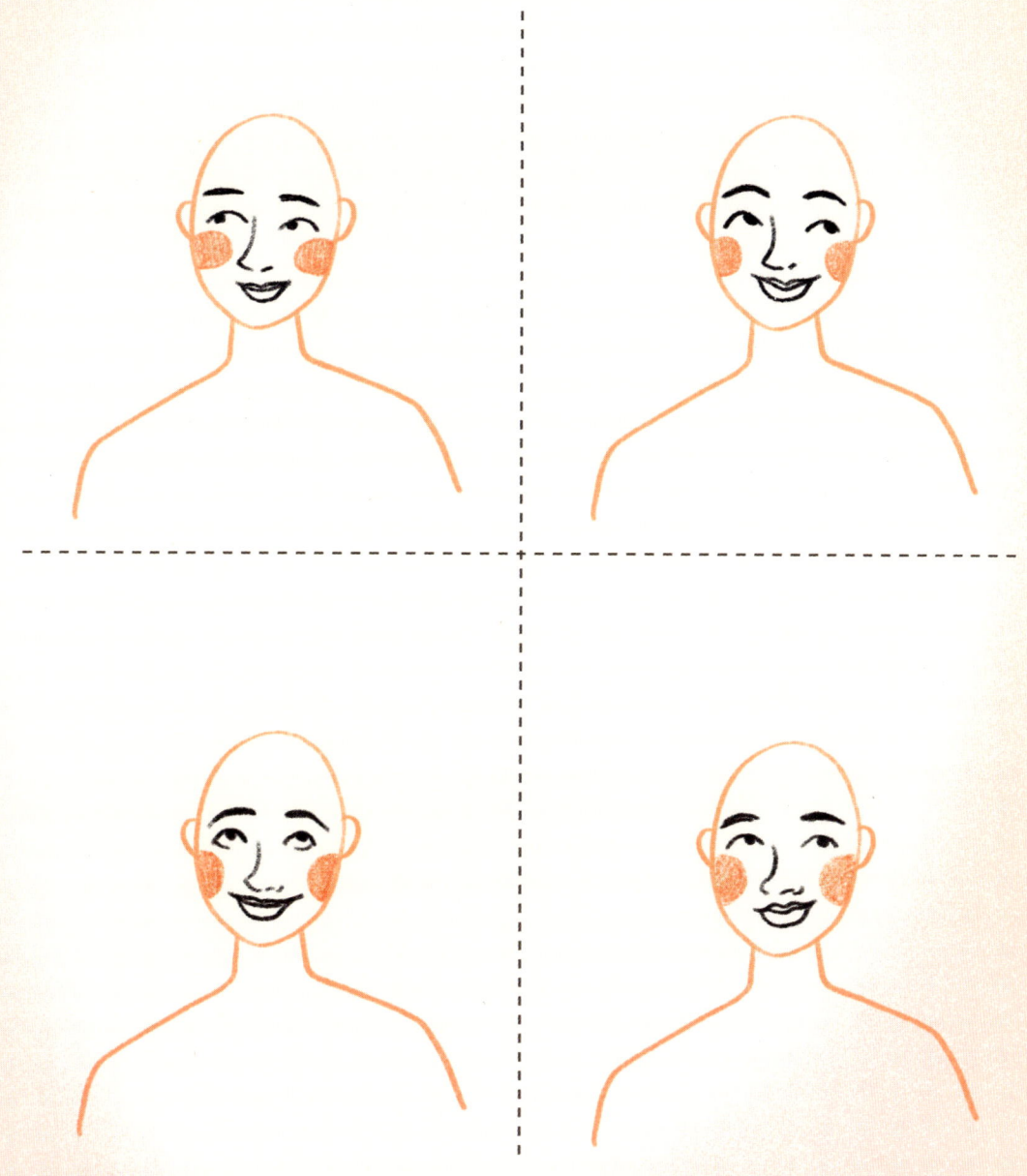

MY CRAZY HAIR DAY

BAD HAIR DAY

Sometimes your hair has its own ideas. Here are some
fun examples of how hair can just do its own thing.

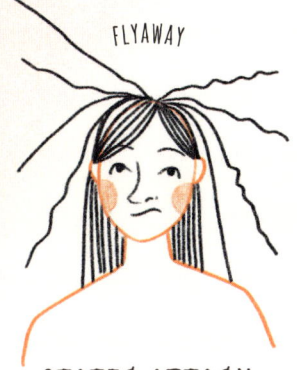

FLYAWAY

STATIC ATTACK

ALL OVER THE PLACE

UNCONTROLLABLE

KEEP IT UNEVEN

DIY FRINGE

ON-END FRINGE

ROGUE BANGS

FULL COVERAGE!

THE VEIL

FLAT TOP, FLUFFY BOTTOM

HAT HAIR

UNFLATTERING CLOUDS

THE POODLE

OUT-OF-PLACE CURL

A LONELY CORKSCREW

SHORT AND FLAT

BOWL CUT

FRAMES & SUNNIES

Whether they're trendy or functional, glasses and sunglasses can completely transform your selfie.

CHOOSE HEART-SHAPED SHADES FOR RETRO CHIC.

INTRODUCE YOUR SELFIE

Now that we know the basics, we can experiment with face outlines, background shapes, pattern and colour. You're unique, so don't be afraid to make your selfie unique, too.

JUST BEING MY SELFIE

PART 3

ENTIRE SELFIE

Nobody is complete without a body,
so love your shape and learn how to draw
it from every angle.

PROPORTIONS

Start with a stick figure, and add shape by padding it out with circles and sausage shapes. Then adjust the outline and scale as you go, selecting features to fit your portrait.

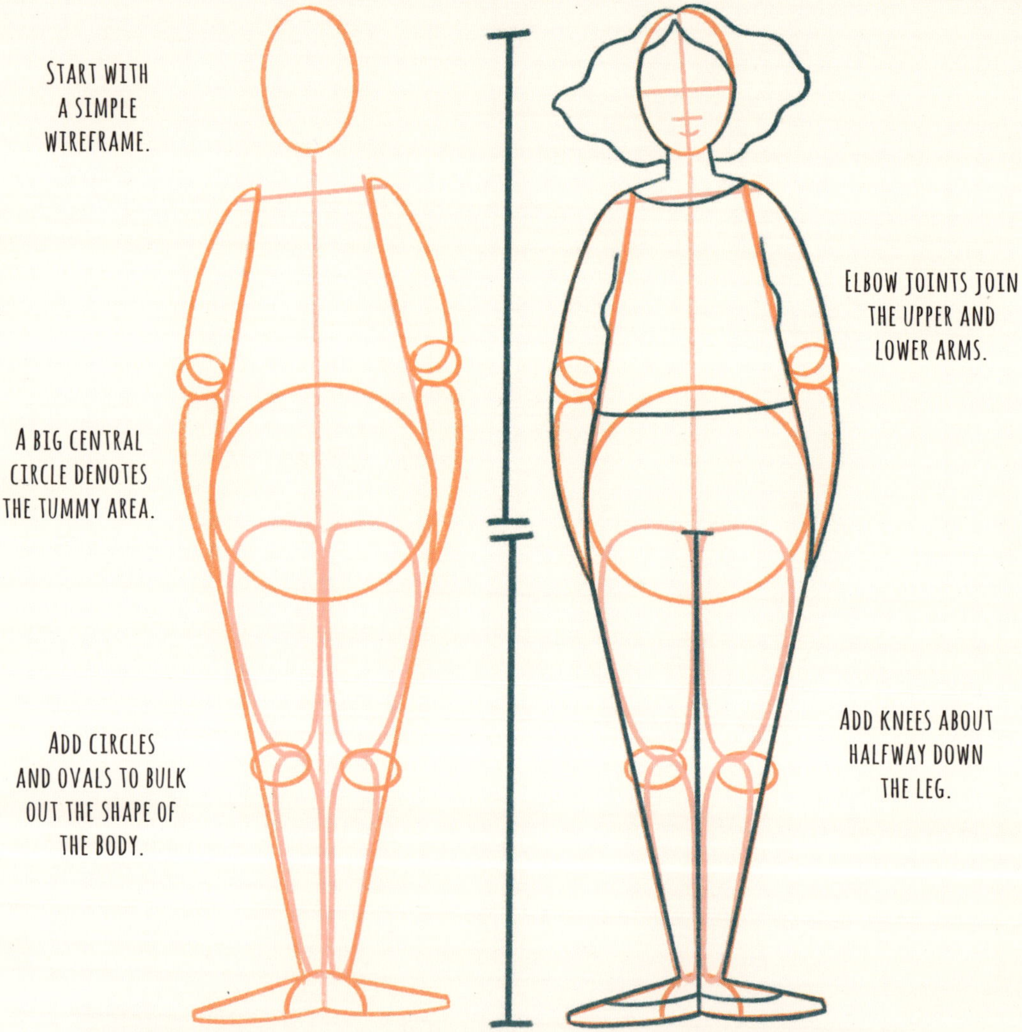

START WITH A SIMPLE WIREFRAME.

ELBOW JOINTS JOIN THE UPPER AND LOWER ARMS.

A BIG CENTRAL CIRCLE DENOTES THE TUMMY AREA.

ADD CIRCLES AND OVALS TO BULK OUT THE SHAPE OF THE BODY.

ADD KNEES ABOUT HALFWAY DOWN THE LEG.

You can tweak the proportions by altering the lengths of certain limbs, changing the size and shape of the figure – for example, making arms larger and curvier, or slimmer and more defined around the shoulder and elbow joints.

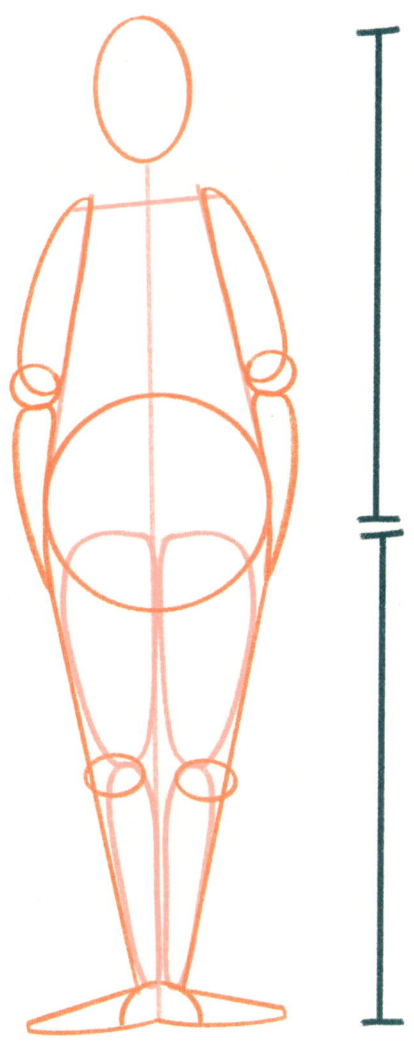

STRETCH OR SHRINK

Now you know the basics of proportion you can experiment with it. Stretching the shapes out will create someone tall and thin, whereas pushing them closer together will create someone short and wide.

HOW TO DRAW HANDS

Hands are one of those drawing hurdles, but hopefully these tips will help you float right over them.

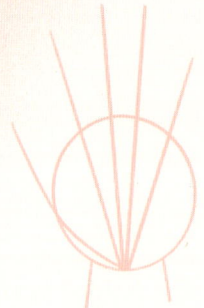  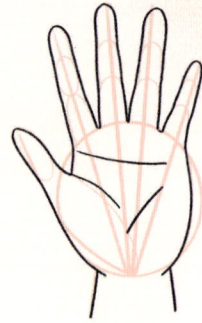

STEP 1:

Start with a circle for your palm. Draw a dot at the bottom, and sketch where your fingers and thumb go to from that point.

STEP 2:

Each finger is made up of three joints and your thumb is made up of two. Build the outlines with simple shapes.

STEP 3:

Draw the outline of the hand around the guide shape and add line detail.

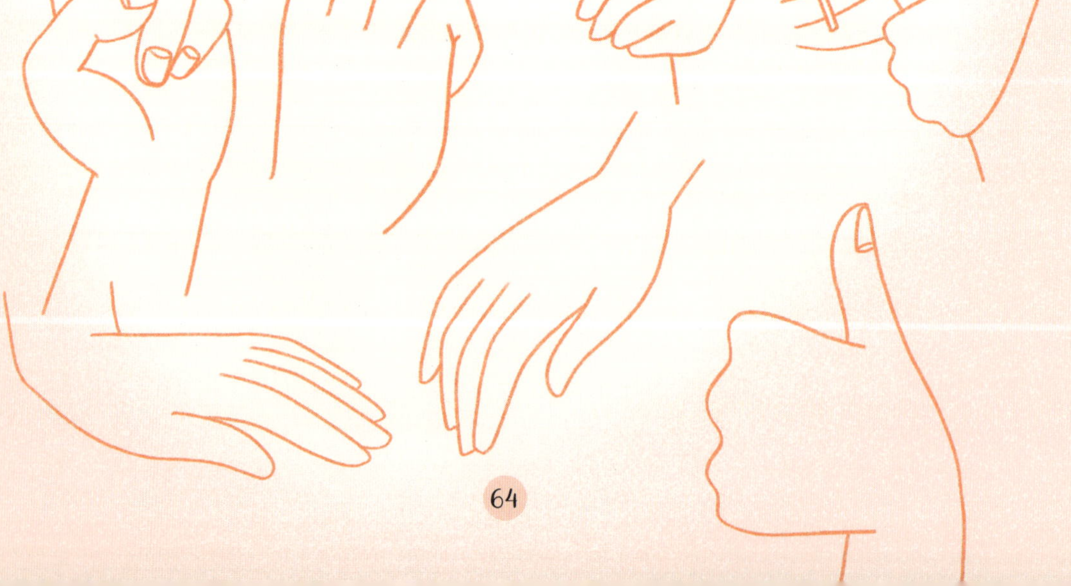

MY HANDS

ANGLES OF YOUR FEET

Practise drawing your feet from
above and from the side.

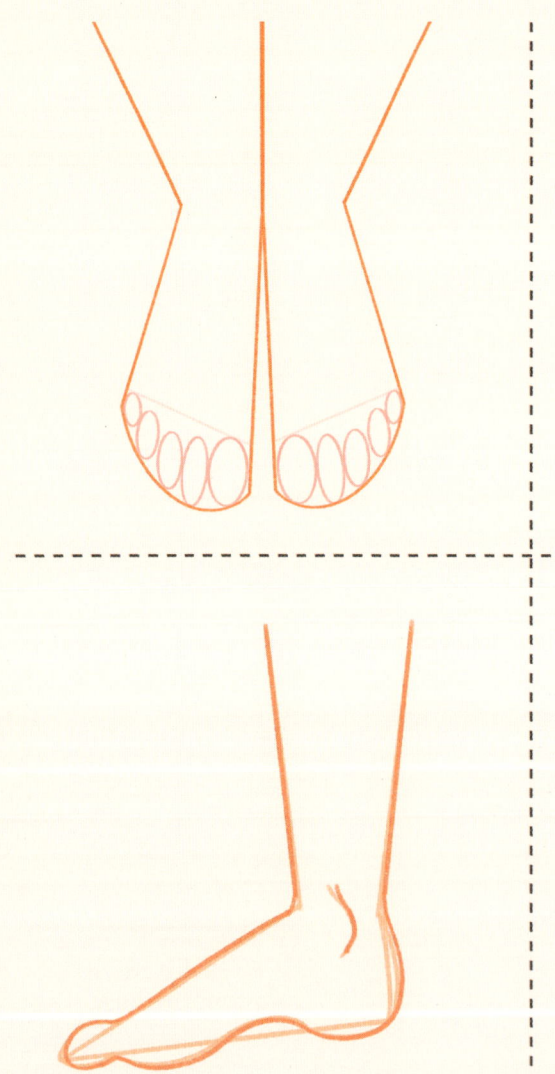

HOW TO DRAW FEET

Feet don't have to be difficult. For a side view, all you need to do is follow these three simple steps. You can even just simplify the shape to a triangle, for a more stylized look, or add some snazzy shoes.

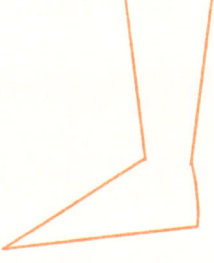

STEP 1:
Start with two lines for the leg, then add a triangle at the bottom for the foot.

STEP 2:
On the bottom line, add a slight arch in the middle and a small bump at the point for the toe.

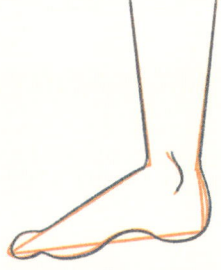

STEP 3:
Create a slight curve at the back for the heel. Draw the outline of the foot around the guide shape and add detail.

ANGLES

There are so many ways to draw feet. Consider drawing them from different angles to make them more interesting.

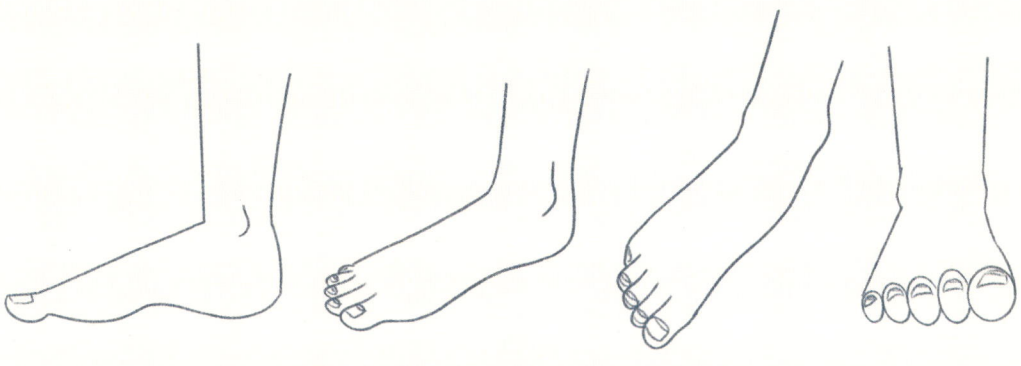

BOOBS, BUMS & TUMS

The key to capturing your body and your
friends' bodies is to not be afraid to give
them some shape, or take some away!

THE SIZE OF YOUR CIRCLES
WILL HELP DETERMINE
HOW VOLUPTUOUS THAT
BUM WILL BE.

DRAW YOUR BODY PARTS

BODY CONFIDENCE

A weightlifting champion doesn't have a set size.

GIVE THE CHEST LESS SHAPE.

USE SMALLER CIRCLES FOR THE JOINTS OF SLIMMER PEOPLE.

USE A CIRCLE TO ADD SHAPE TO THE STOMACH.

USE THE BOTTOM HALF OF THE TUMMY CIRCLE TO GIVE SHAPE TO THE THIGHS.

STANCE

Adjust your standing stances to give your drawings more character.
Try a relaxed, hand-on-hip gesture or a power stance.

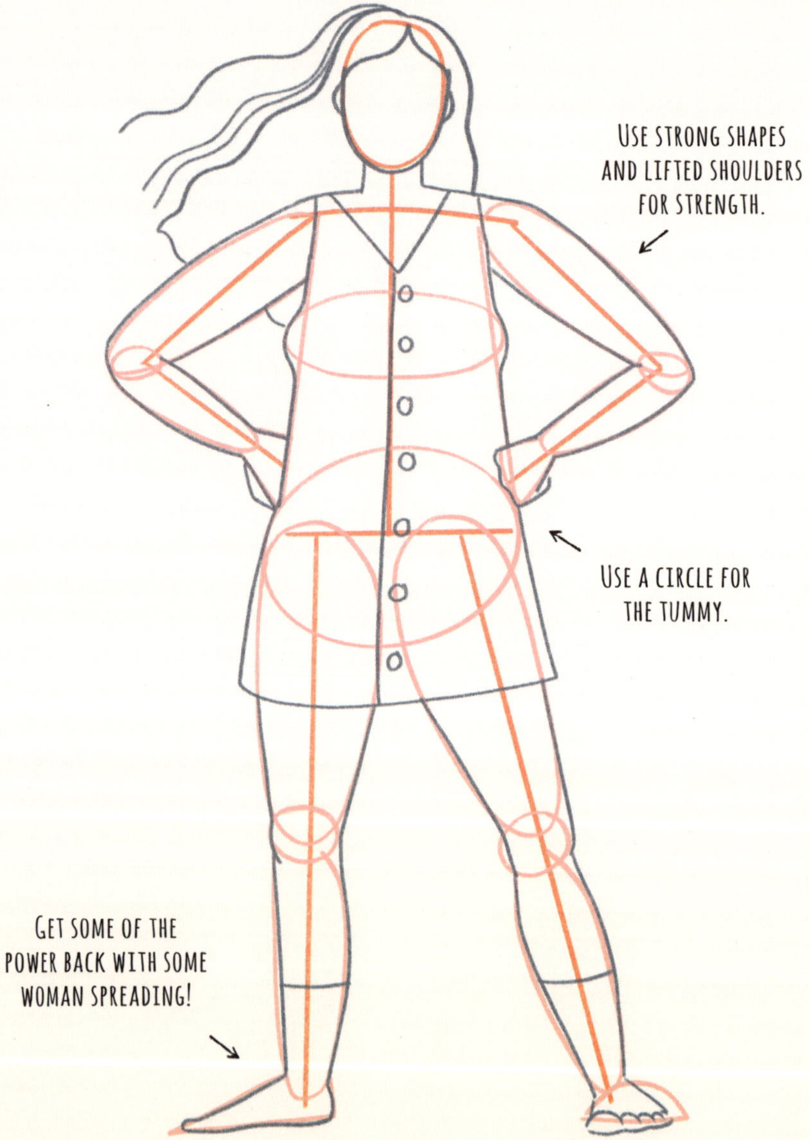

USE STRONG SHAPES
AND LIFTED SHOULDERS
FOR STRENGTH.

USE A CIRCLE FOR
THE TUMMY.

GET SOME OF THE
POWER BACK WITH SOME
WOMAN SPREADING!

EXPERIMENT WITH THE
WIREFRAME TO ACHIEVE
DIFFERENT POSES.

ADJUST THE
LINE OF THE SPINE.

DRAW THE HAND
ON THE HIP FOR
A CASUAL POSE.

THINK ABOUT
BENDS AT THE
KNEES AND ELBOWS.

CONSIDER THE
POSITION OF THE FEET.

ACTION SHOT

Draw you and your friends playing your favourite sport. Think of how the figures might interact and the positioning of their limbs as they play.

SPORTS DAY

Now you know how to draw an active stance, drawing people playing different sports will be easy. Position the bat for the perfect tennis swing or get those arms in the air to duck that ball!

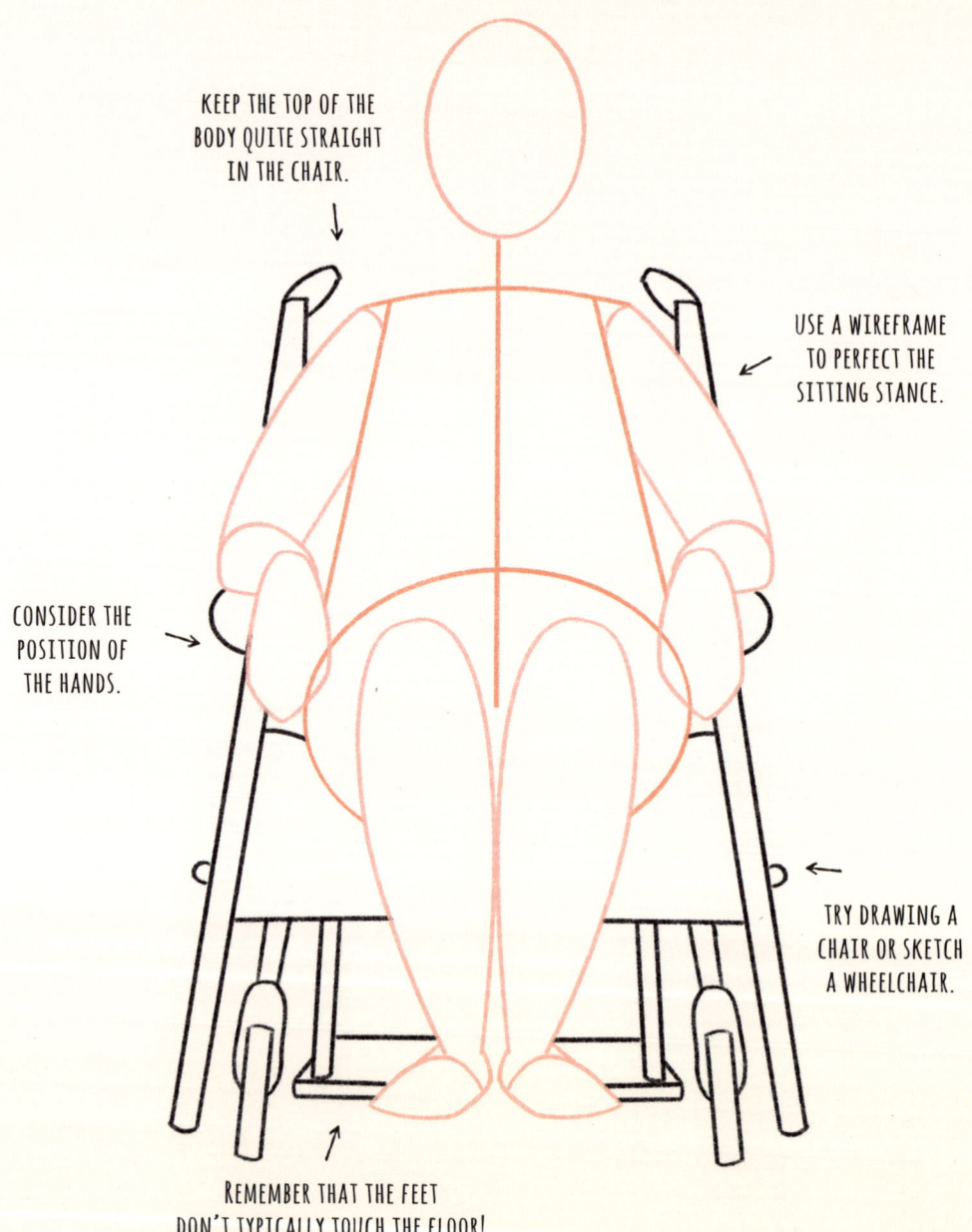

KEEP THE TOP OF THE
BODY QUITE STRAIGHT
IN THE CHAIR.

USE A WIREFRAME
TO PERFECT THE
SITTING STANCE.

CONSIDER THE
POSITION OF
THE HANDS.

TRY DRAWING A
CHAIR OR SKETCH
A WHEELCHAIR.

REMEMBER THAT THE FEET
DON'T TYPICALLY TOUCH THE FLOOR!

SITTING & RECLINING

Drawing a sitting position is a little more challenging, but starting with a wireframe first will help you to get the position right.

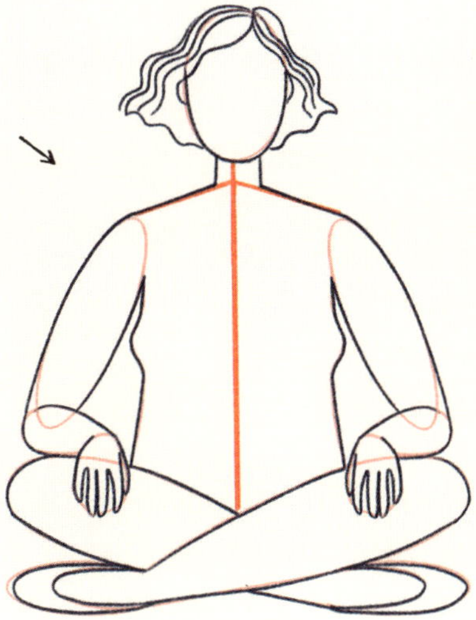

CROSSED LEGS ARE PERFECT FOR MEDITATING FIGURES.

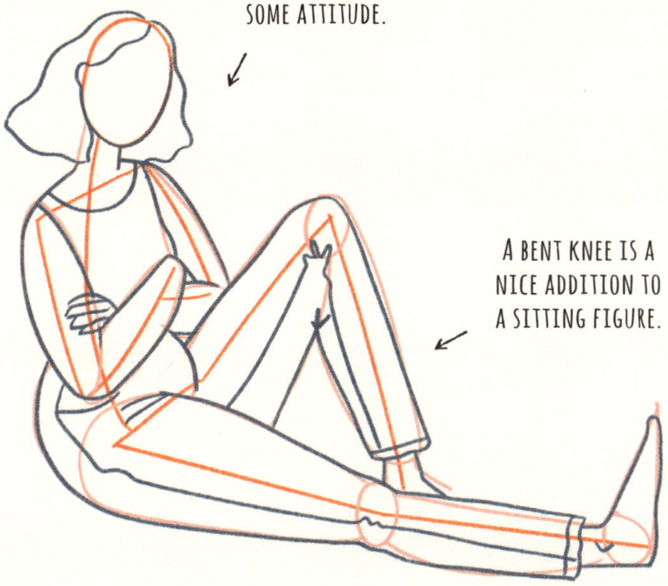

CROSS THE ARMS FOR SOME ATTITUDE.

A BENT KNEE IS A NICE ADDITION TO A SITTING FIGURE.

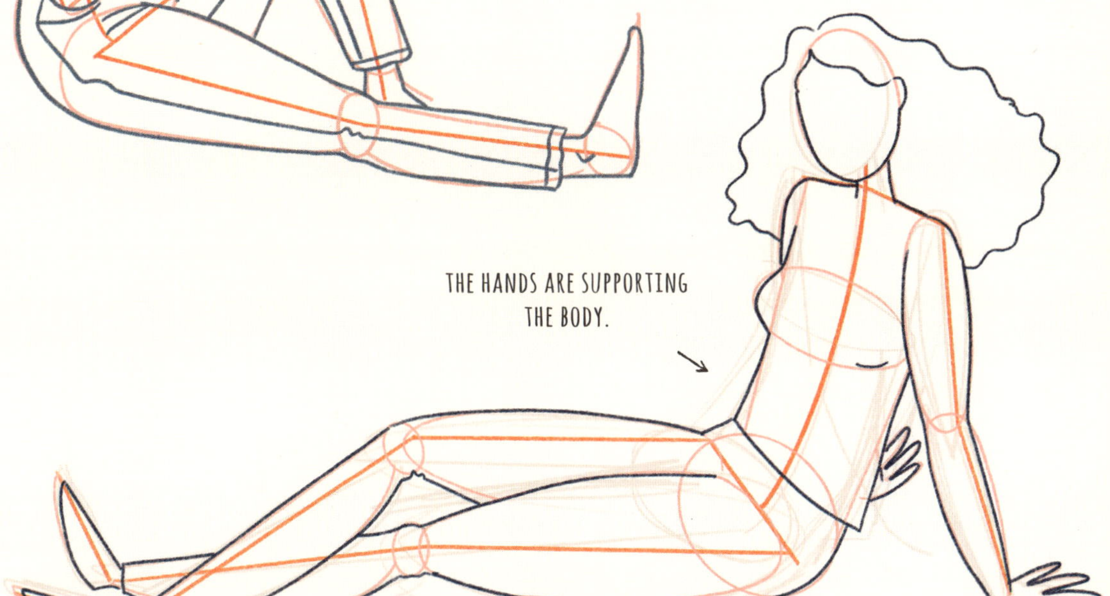

THE HANDS ARE SUPPORTING THE BODY.

SITTING

If your characters are sitting in a chair or
in a wheelchair, try looking up some images
for reference first. This will help you to master
the different elements of the chair.

Draw your figure lazing on a beach
or chilling in a chair.

DRESSING ROOM

Adjusting lengths can turn trousers into cropped jeans or shorts, and altering the shape of a skirt can take it from a floating boho style to a formal A-line or pencil. Remember to let the personality of the different characters shine through in their clothing choices.

MAKEOVER!

Give this group of friends the outfits of their dreams.
Add details to the trousers, create texture or pattern on the
tops or bottoms, and use lots of colour.

Get these partygoers ready by drawing the rest of their outfits. Fill them with colour and pattern.

ACCESSORIZE

Finish these selfies by adding faces
and drawing their clothing.

PILE MOST OF THE SCARF
ON TOP OF THE HEAD.

USE BOLD COLOURS
AND PATTERN.

USE DIFFERENT TONES TO SHOW THE
DIFFERENT PARTS OF THE SCARF.

GO VINTAGE.

A HAT FOR EVERY OCCASION

Draw a hat for when you are. . .

Skiing

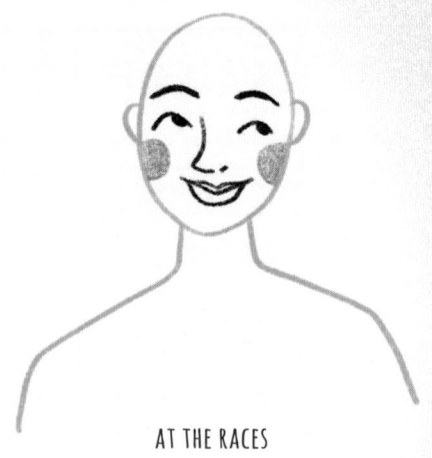

AT THE RACES

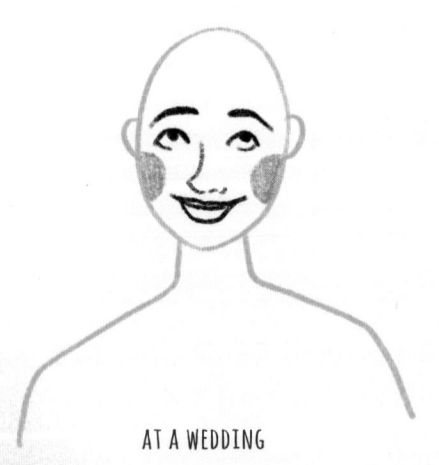

AT A WEDDING

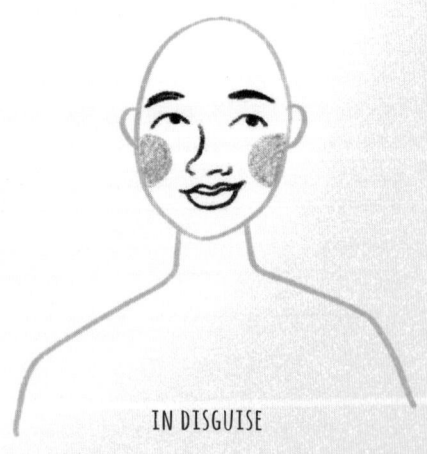

IN DISGUISE

ACCESSORIZE

Draw your dream bonnets, beanies, top hats and summer hats.

PAY ATTENTION
TO THE RIM.

ADD A BOW FOR
DECORATION.

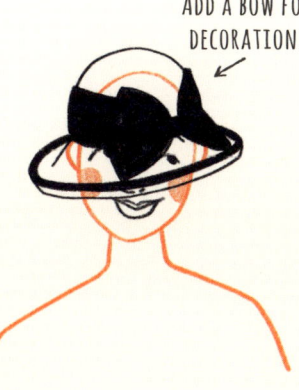

SIMPLE LINES
CONVEY TEXTURE.

ADD TRIM AND
JEWELS TO YOUR CROWN.

CURVING LINES AND A THICK
BAND CREATE THIS CLASSIC.

ACCESSORIZE

Give your selfie some bold statement earrings
or an artfully placed stud.

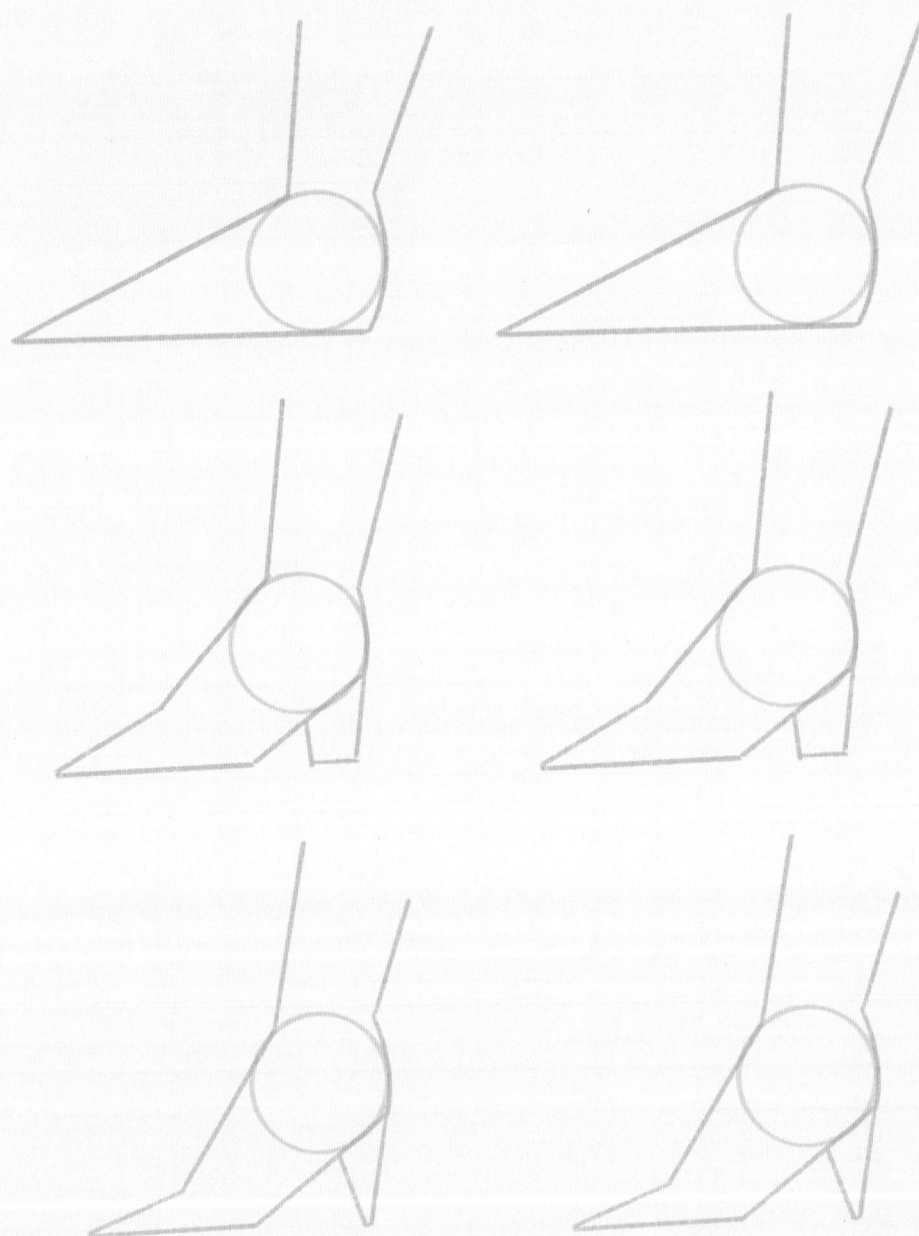

SHOES, GLORIOUS SHOES!

Drawing some flashy footwear doesn't have to be difficult – just follow the simple outlines opposite.

STYLISH
BROGUES

COMFY TRAINERS

STRAPPY
SANDALS

BOLD BLOCK
HEELS

CLASSIC
HIGH HEELS

CHELSEA BOOTS

SCARS & TATTOOS

Whether it is a beauty mark, a spattering of freckles, a scar, or a tattoo, everyone has a defining mark that makes them unique.

92

MY ENTIRE SELFIE

PART 4
SELFIE STYLE

Whether you want to be in monochrome or
full colour, an animal or a flower, a robot
or a mermaid – now's the time to let your
imagination run wild!

BLACK & WHITE

Create your own graphic novel character by drawing your selfie throughout the day in the four spaces opposite.

SHADED STYLE

MORNING

MIDDAY

EVENING

NIGHT

MONOCHROME

Using a monochromatic colour is a good drawing challenge. Pick a light, medium and dark shade of one colour and draw your selfies, introducing different textures into your image to create contrast.

SMUDGED CIRCLES    CROSS-HATCHING    SPONGED EFFECT

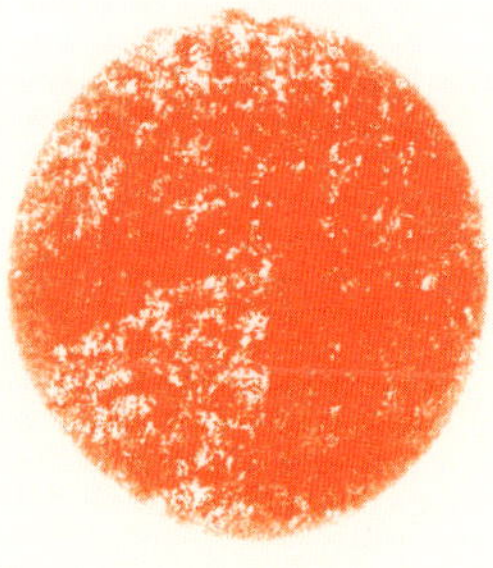

DIFFERENT TONES

FULL COLOUR

Don't be afraid to experiment with colour, but give yourself
a palette to work with so you don't overdo it. Less is more.

YOUR NATURAL COLOURING

YOUR FANTASY COLOURING

POP-ART SELFIE

Try your own pop-art selfie by drawing your portrait in these four frames.

POP ART

Channel Andy Warhol! The key to the pop-art portrait is to churn out multiple versions of one image in various bold colour combinations.

PATTERN OVERLOAD!

Pick three or four colours and practise drawing
simple patterns on these swatches:

POLKA DOT

PLAID

PINSTRIPE

FLORAL

GEOMETRIC

ANIMAL

BEHAVIOUR PATTERNS

PICK A PRINT

Choose the patterns that best represent the personalities of four of your friends and draw their portraits here.

I, ROBOT

Draw the blueprint for your robot selfie here. Are you
a futuristic or vintage robot? What are you made out of?
What are your special robot capabilities?

MERMAID

Draw your selfie on this mermaid silhouette, adding your hair, skin tone, sea-themed crown and tail details.

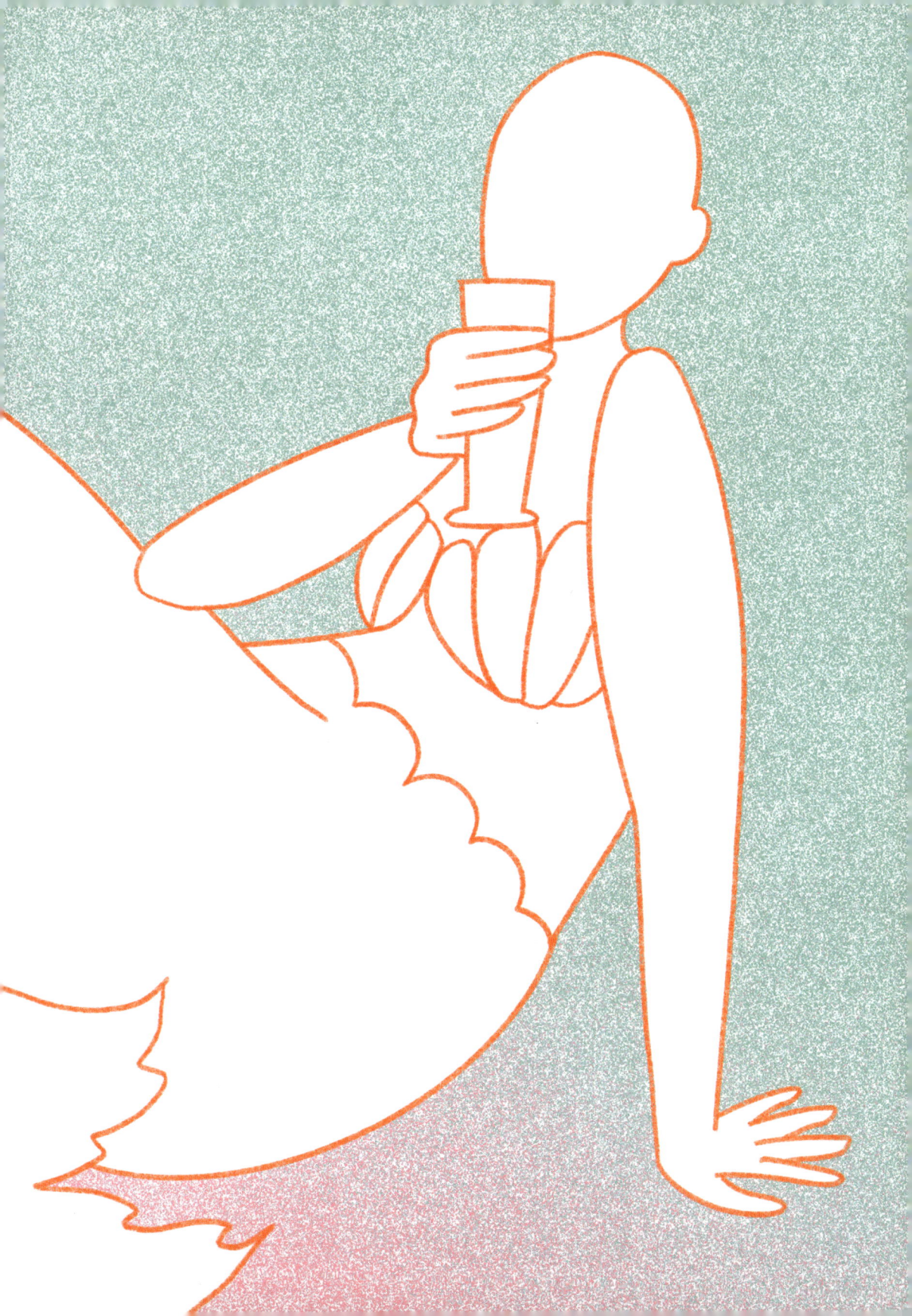

 # LIFE UNDER THE SEA

Recreate yourself and your crew in an underwater world.

HOW KAWAII AM I?

CHIBI: KAWAII!

Chibi is a Japanese style of drawing people and animals in a small, cute way.

BIG HEADS

WIDE EYES

SMALL BODIES

TINY FEET

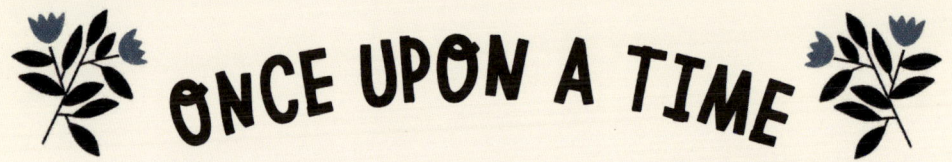

ONCE UPON A TIME

Think about fun new ways to illustrate the cover
of your favourite book. Don't forget to include the title!

ALICE IN WONDERLAND

LITERARY LADY

Draw yourself as your favourite
fictional character from a book.

SUPER YOU!

Think about a random talent that you have. Make your uniform your favourite colour and include your superhero logo. Add special functionality, accessories and a sidekick.

DREAM TEAM

Finish the drawing of the superheroes below by adding fierce faces, and decorating their outfits with logos representing their superpowers.

122

FLOWER POWER

Flower crowns are the perfect accessory for creating the ultimate selfie. Draw your selfie in the flower crown below.

What if your friends were flowers? Draw their portraits on these stems and frame their faces with their favourite blooms.

ANIMAL SELFIE

If you have always wanted a cat or have a pet pooch that you adore, an animal makeover is the perfect thing to try. Add ears and whiskers, and draw yourself wearing animal-print clothing.

MY ANIMAL SIDE

HIPPIE OR VINTAGE CHIC?

This is your chance to give yourself a retro makeover - are you a lover of the flapper dress or more of a boho type?

MY VINTAGE SELFIE

SO RETRO

Draw your friends in throwback fashions.

RETRO CLASSICS

Give yourself a pink wig for disco chic, or get
inspired by Audrey Hepburn and pair an LBD with
some bubbly in hand.

132

COOL GIRL

Whether it's rocking out at a gig or hopping onto a motorbike, some girls just ooze cool.

TRY OUT A PINK PERM.

CAPTURE THAT LOOK.

WEAR SOME COOL GLASSES.

THE MAN FILTER

Have some fun with funky facial hair
and masculine accessories.

135

PHOTO BOOTH

Photo booths are the ideal place to capture moments
with friends, making funny faces and gestures.

FACE PAINT

Creating face-painted looks can be a fun challenge,
from getting festival-ready with glittery designs to
adorning your favourite beast with fur markings.

GIVE THESE FACES A MAGICAL MAKEOVER

GLAMAZONS

Make-up can give you a lovely, dewy glow or take you to the extreme, so it's fun to experiment with this in your drawings. Add character to your sketches with heavy eyeliner and glossy lips.